SPEAK

TO MY

HEALING

HABAKKUK COOPER

SPEAK to MY HEALING

Published by Habakkuk Cooper (Self Publisher)
Oluchi Coaching and Consulting, LLC
Copyright © 2023 Habakkuk Cooper
Visit: www.oluchicoachingandconsulting.com
ISBN Print: 979-8-9866001-0-9
ISBN eBook: 979-8-9866001-2-3
Library of Congress Control Number: 2022923032

Disclaimer

Every attempt has been made to source all quotes properly.
Cover Art: Victoria Ross
Cover Design: Victoria Ross
Formatting and Interior Design: Brandon Evans
Printed in the United States of America
First Edition 2023

DEDICATION

I would like to dedicate this book to my beautiful and loving daughter Tiki" and granddaughter "Aari", who are the reasons that I developed the courage and strength to never give up. Your unconditional love, encouragement, and support have helped me through many challenging times. You guys are my main motivation to be a better woman. I love you guys so much!

To my beautiful sister, Asha-I admire you, your strength, and your love. When I needed to talk, you were always there for me, even when you couldn't be there for yourself. I Love you

And to my beautiful mother-Thank you for bringing me into this world...I love you

To all of those who need healing, I am praying for you. You will be okay because God loves you. Sending lots of love your way.

-Love, Habakkuk

TABLE OF CONTENTS

INTRODUCTION

W e learn our true self, our true identity when we first understand who created us and why. Angel Muse wanted to learn her true self, as she attempted to live her life by these affirmations:

- ✦ I am a Genuine Soul
- ✦ I am Perfectly Imperfect
- ✦ I am Kind, Caring, Loving, Nurturing, and Giving
- ✦ I am a Steward of God who loves to help others
- ✦ I am True to myself and others
- ✦ I am a Woman with a voice who needs to be heard
- ✦ I am a God-Fearing Woman

These powerful words have always been Angel's foundation and what has sustained her through life's ups and downs as a young adult and into adulthood. Yet, she did not always remember them amidst her abandonment, fear, anxiety, hurt, and pain. Who was she without the pain? Could her life be worthwhile? Could she live a life healed? These are questions Angel would ask herself time and time again.

This story is the everyday reality of a young Black girl who is starved for love, affection, and protection from a father and mother. Unfortunately, these needs were met temporarily by Angel's teenage vices. Angel experienced the harsh and undeserved pain that comes from divorced parents, the rejection of a wicked stepmom, the heartbreak of love lost, the agony of rape and denied justice from the legal system, the repercussions of wrong choices, and the challenges of single motherhood. This was the painful reality of her life.

This is not another book on healing. It is a book about the journey of a young girl broken by the absence of and lack of love from a man who was her father but never fulfilled his role. It is a journey of learning how to become a woman and to see the value within herself. Angel did not know her identity or how to truly love herself, so she resorted to seeing her lesser self. Unfortunately, her life choices followed suit.

Although there was hope, the hope that Angel sought after, and subsequently found, was not within herself but in whom God had created and called her to be.

Angel's healing process began with deciding to be better, letting go of past hurts, and learning to forgive.

Is there hope? Yes! This author has proven that it doesn't matter how bad you have had it in life; it is not the end of your story. You can become better by God's grace.

Angel's story is one of yesterday's failures becoming stepping stones to a better future. Her story is your story.

Speak to My Healing

Chapter One

FAMILY TIES

CHILDHOOD

The Southside of Chicago was where Angel called home. Born to Willie, a small business owner of an auto repair shop, and Cheryl, a stay-at-home mother, Angel remembers a somewhat happy life with her parents and siblings. Growing up in Chicago made Angel a tough little girl who had to fight every day on her way to school and on the way back home. Although she was teased at school about her frail body frame and dark-skinned complexion, she could hold her own. She had to learn how to fight or be crushed by the influences on the streets. The home was a safe place for her where she had a loving mother who made sure that she was there to feed her soul with motivation and give love with open arms. Her childhood was filled with happy moments of caring family and friends. There was always family around who loved to barbecue and throw parties regularly. Playing outside every day was Angel's favorite thing to do. She would often skate around the neighborhood or play Double Dutch with her friends and was known as one of the best Double Dutch jumpers on her block. "No one can out-jumpAngel," was the word on the street in the neighborhood. Recess was her favorite time at school since she knew that this was when everyone would come out with their jump ropes to challenge who would be the best jumper for that day. Those were some fun times! Life was good…until it wasn't.

Little Girl Lost

Angel's mother, Cheryl, was (and still is) a loving and caring mother. She made sure she was home before and after school to see her children and told them every day about how much they were loved. Cheryl lacked love and affection from her mother, Angel's estranged grandmother, so she never wanted her children to experience the same lack of affection. Cheryl wanted her children to be close to each other, so she made sure they did lots of things together while having each other's backs no matter what. Chicago streets were no joke, so being close as a family meant everything. Whenever there was an argument or fight between the siblings, Angel's mother would make them apologize to one another immediately and hug her. On the flip side, when there was a fight between a sibling and a stranger, Angel's mother's favorite words to another sibling who was on the scene were…" so did you help? Because if you didn't you better go back, or we're going to be fighting". Cheryl did not play about her children abandoning one another during rough times. Everything in life that was valuable to Angel or meant anything to her stemmed from what Angel learned from her mother. It was from her that Angel learned to be a strong woman while also showing kindness to anyone who needed it, and she always had the desire to help others in any way she could.

Angel didn't see much of her father while her parents were married. He owned a small car repair shop business and spent most of his time banging on cars to earn an honest living. He was a workaholic. That little shop on 89th and Ashland was truly the place that Willie called home. Even though they co-existed under the same roof, Angel didn't see much of her father, and she didn't get the love and affection that she yearned for from a father-which were necessary ingredients during a child's growth period.

Angel had no memories of hugs and kisses from her father or the words, "I love you!" Eventually, her parents divorced when she was five years old, which caused her and her siblings to have an even deeper hole in each their hearts. Even before the divorce was final, the family quickly separated into different homes. After the divorce, Angel remembers that her father would promise to pick up her and her siblings to spend time together, but he would rarely show up. Instead, he'd leave them on the front porch fully dressed in their winter coats, waiting endlessly for his arrival. They eagerly hoped that he would finally show up just one time, even after all the disappointments. This continuously selfish act forced their mom to make the final decision to stop preparing them for the hopes of an honest and loving father. She had finally realized that this was too much for her young children's hearts to bear.

Even on those days when Willie didn't show up to spend time with his kids, they still desired his love and attention. Angel desired to be a "daddy's" girl who was unyielding and refused to give up on her daddy. She would wait on that porch for hours after her mother and siblings had already gone inside. Even as a little girl, Angel always saw the good in people, so she believed in giving second, third, and even fourth chances; she tried to stay positive because maybe one day, her father would realize that his children were the best things that had ever happened to him. Eventually, Willie would get around to picking them up to spend the weekend or the summer with him. At times, he would pick them up and bring them to his home, where he had already established another family with an even younger new wife and two kids.

Being in her father's new home caused Angel uncomfortable, not necessarily because of her father, but because of his new wife, Angel's stepmom, Bianca. Bianca was at least 20 years younger than Angel's dad, and her age made it awkward between her and Angel's older siblings. She made it clear that she was not interested in being a stepmom to Angel and her siblings or playing any kind of role in their lives. Angel hated being in their home because she sensed that Bianca hated having them there. Her eyes and body language told it all.

The Wicked Stepmother

Bianca and Willie had two children together, and they seemed to get more attention from both Willie and Bianca than Angel and her siblings ever did. Angel could never understand why. Bianca had the luxury of being a stay-at-home mom who would use her husband's money to buy clothes from expensive stores for her children, but never nice clothes for Angel and her siblings. Angel and her sibling's clothes were always purchased from thrift stores. Any visit to her stepmom meant mistreatment for her and her siblings. She demeaned them and separated them from her children because she considered them as being "bad influences". Angel remembered a time when she slapped her sister just for playing in the snow. There was always something that set Bianca off when Angel and her siblings would visit. Bianca emotionally mistreated Angel and her siblings, making them feel devalued and unworthy of themselves and the better things in life. The glaring looks from her stepmom made them feel as though they were the cast-off children created from outside of their marriage, even though they were there before Bianca and her children.

When Angel's stepmother didn't want to be bothered, she would send only Angel and her siblings to their father's shop just to sit there. To her, they were an inconvenience in her life. Surprisingly, Angel was okay with this gesture since the only thing that mattered to her was to spend time with her father. She just wanted his love and attention; she wanted her daddy.

There were several occasions when Bianca saw Angel and her siblings as nothing but menaces. She questioned their visits and treated them as pests. Her stepmom even dared to tell Angel's mother that she didn't want them there because it was too much for her to deal with. Angel's mom was in hardship at the time, and struggling to make ends meet. She would ask Angel's father for financial support for the children, but it fell on deaf ears. Despite his lack of financial support, Cheryl made sure that her children still had regular visits with their father to maintain their relationship. No mother ever wants her children to be considered a nuisance, especially by their father's new wife.

Angel's stepmom didn't want them around and it was obvious to everyone. Hence, the weekends and summers only got worse and more isolated. It seemed Angel's father didn't care about his kid's well-being or feelings. For him, their presence at his home was just to fulfill a sense of righteousness, like a "Hey, got them for the weekend, so I've done my fatherly duty"-even though his presence was nonexistent.

Truly an Angel

Bianca's best friend, Annette, was Heaven sent into Angel's life. She was by her and her siblings' side during the tough times of visiting their father's home. The moment Annette realized Angel and her siblings were with their stepmom, she would immediately pick them up from Bianca's home to bring them to her home so that they could experience some time of normality and happiness. Annette had a home in Country Club Hills—a nice suburban area outside of

Chicago. Her home was beautiful with a huge backyard where children could happily play. Most importantly, she had a loving and nurturing heart that Angel would never forget.

Angel felt Annette saved her from Bianca's emotional and mental torture. Annette was Angel's guardian angel. She saw what was going on and without question protected her and her siblings. When they were with her, they didn't have to say anything because their eyes were the mirror of their broken souls. She never spoke about the things that were inflicted upon them by her best friend Bianca. Despite the continuous mistreatment, not once did she speak badly about her best friend. Rather, she did what God instructed her to do which was to help them in their time of need, and she did it quite well. She was indeed their Godsent.

Sadly, Angel's daddy became good at ignoring her and her siblings. Their presence didn't matter because his focus was always on fixing cars. On their visitation weekends, they had no choice but to spend that time at their father's car repair shop just to be able to spend time with him. As early as 8 a.m., Angel and her siblings would get dropped off at their father's car repair shop her day consisted of just sitting in the shop and waiting on him to finish. When they were hungry, Angel's father would give them some money to walk about three blocks to the nearest shop to buy potato chips and candy to hold them over until he finished his work at the shop. This became the normal routine for them. It seemed easy for Angel's dad to focus his attention on objects because he didn't know how to love or focus on people.

Angel always wondered why her father was more interested in working on his cars than spending time with his kids. She wasn't at an age to understand or try to understand her father's struggles. All she knew was that she and her siblings tried to get him to love them to no avail. Anger and resentment were the only emotions that consumed Angel's heart and mind.

The only person who cared for Angel and her siblings whenever she visited her father's home was Annette, Bianca's best friend. In her mind, no one else cared how they were being treated, and this made her sad.

Feelings of Resentment

Angel yearned for attention and affection from her father, but she would later understand why her father disappeared into his own shadow of trauma. After all, Willie's mother and father abandoned and disowned him at a very young age. Many years passed and Angel began to develop a trauma in her heart that grew from the absence of her father, both physically, mentally, and emotionally. She would watch other fathers holding hands with their daughters and spending time together, while overwhelming feelings of pain, hurt, and sadness would consume her. Angel always imagined having a father who would hold her hand, hug her, kiss her, and to one day walk her down the aisle to give her away to a man who would love her unconditionally. What a fantasy that was!

People always labeled Angel as overly emotional, because she cried almost every time at the sight of any father-daughter interaction between strangers. After all, she wanted that type of relationship with her father so badly. The only time that Angel felt close to having a good time with her father was when he would take them to McDonald's as a treat. McDonald's was the place that made all the kids happy- like Disney World. This may have been his way of letting them know that he loved them. Although he never showed his emotions in front of his children, Angel believed that her father enjoyed seeing his children happy on those rare McDonald's visits. In hopes of there being a stitch of love there, Angel continued to hold on to her daddy for dear life.

Angel had harbored a lot of hurt and resentment because she watched her father treat his other children better. She didn't know whether to love or hate them, even though it wasn't their fault.

Her half-siblings appeared to be very privileged, while her mother struggled to keep a roof over Angel and her siblings' heads. Cheryl used public assistance to feed them with no help from her father. As she got older, Angel would be embarrassed at the mere fact of having to go to the store with a book of food stamps in her hand to purchase food. Meanwhile, her stay-at-home stepmother lived in a big beautiful home and was able to enroll her children, Angel's half-siblings, into private school, give them piano lessons and gymnastics classes, and to top it all off, take numerous trips to Disney World. It seemed as if they got all the best of him, and Angel and her siblings got the leftovers or nothing at all.

It wasn't fair that they got to live a good life, while Angel and her siblings suffered financially just a few miles away. This traumatized Angel. Angel carried this same resentment toward her half-siblings because they were connected to her step-mom. Could you blame her for feeling this way? She was only reacting to what life had dealt her.

Any outsider could see that it was obvious that it wasn't their fault that Angel's father treated her and her siblings differently because he was no longer married to their mother. She just couldn't understand why life was so unfair to her and her siblings, yet, her half-siblings had it handed to them on a silver platter.

Even in all this partial treatment, a part of her loved her half-siblings because they were also a part of her. Like it or not, they were still family. They were her blood, and most importantly, they were innocent children themselves.

Despite the flawed family dynamics, Angel decided to develop good relationships with them, but that relationship wouldn't last long.

Chapter Two

BROKEN PROMISES

Mommy Starts Over

Angel's mom had a new man in her life, John, whom she fell in love with and eventually married. He was a good man to her and kind to Angel and her siblings. Angel couldn't imagine someone having a big enough heart to take on a woman with five children, but John did.

John was a hard-working man, construction being his trade. Every time he got paid, he would give Cheryl every dime of his check. Happiness had finally found her, but unfortunately, it wouldn't last forever. Angel's stepfather, John, was the opposite of Angel's biological father because he was loving and kind; he accepted them and took care of her and her family. When he and her mother married, John moved in and took over the bills while her mother remained a stay-at-home mom. He went to work, came home, and would cook. John was a very good cook. He made Angel feel like she was in a real family—putting together family functions for everyone to enjoy. Angel believed that John loved her mother very much, but he would later become her downfall.

Several years went by, and Angel's mom decided that Chicago was no longer a good place to raise her children. The gangs in Chicago were getting worse to the point that they had started to recruit Angel and her older brother. One day, the gangster disciples (known as GD), dared to come to their home demanding that she and her brother join their gang. Mom was fed up! She was so mad that she came outside with her pistol shouting, "If you'll don't get from in front of my house, I'm going to light up every one of you motherf%$ers." She pointed that gun directly at them. They left Angel's front yard that evening but threatened to return. Angel never forgot her mother's courage that day. And it was also her last memory of Chicago. Angel's mom knew that they needed to leave the city. So, she immediately packed them up and decided to move to Dallas, Texas. John had gotten a job in Dallas, so it made sense for the whole family to move.

While living in Chicago, Angel had many friends, but she there was one particular friend who stood out-her best friend, Lynneice, a.k.a "Neicy". The thought of leaving her best friend, Neicy, other close friends, and cousins behind in Chicago devastated Angel, but she had no choice. Angel felt helpless and scared about what her future would look like, and how her relationship with her father would change. She had to say goodbye to what was once her entire world, but what would she be welcoming into her life in this new state?

The drive to Dallas was long, and Angel spent much of her time staring out of the car window. She admired the beautiful scenery of homes and perfectly made green trees. It was unlike anything she was used to seeing in Chicago. "Wow," she thought. "This is going to be an amazing place!" As they continued to pass by the beautifully manicured lawns of homes that looked like they belong to doctors, lawyers, or even politicians, she felt like they were the Jeffersons, moving on up. That thought quickly disappeared, however, as they pulled up to what looked like an old raggedy shack. Was this the place where they were going live? Would life just look the same as it did in Chicago—insufficient? Angel was so confused as to why her mom would accept living like this after moving from a nice townhome on the upper south side of Chicago.

As the family stood outside of that run-down shack, Angel thought that it couldn't get any worse than that. But it did. When they stepped inside, they found holes in the floor that was so big that if they made a wrong turn, they would be on the ground outside. At night, she would hear creepy noises while sleeping on the bare floor. It was cold and dark. Angel couldn't believe that her loving stepfather had brought them to this devastation. Angel's mother was not the type to say much of anything, so she just made the best of a bad situation. Angel resented that her mother was always so complacent. She could have done bad all by herself.

During this difficult time, Angel's mother would send them back to their father's home for months at a time until she could provide a better living situation for them. Angel dreaded the idea of going back to her father's home because it was never a good experience when Angel went back to Chicago. Once they went back to Chicago, the mistreatment from Bianca continued. Angel's mother knew how she treated them and wouldn't continue to tolerate it, so one day, she decided to threaten to beat up Bianca on site.

Just like the broken house, Cheryl and John's relationship also needed repair. They argued a lot. Little did Angel know that her mom had been keeping a secret about John having an affair while they were in Chicago and that it led to an outside child. Angel's mom had just found out that John had invited his mistress and their baby to Dallas so that he could have easier access to them. The nerve of that man!

Living in Dallas was very difficult for Angel since it consisted of times when there was no food to eat, sleeping on bare, cold hardwood floors, and a lack of proper clothing during the winter months. In the winter, they nearly froze because there was no heat in the home. With thin walls and old, broken, and unstable floors, that home wasn't fit for animals let alone a family. And to add insult to injury, John would disappear from time to time, which led Angel's mother to have to find ways on her own to feed her children. It appeared as though John had slipped into his world of selfishness, and had given up on Angel and her family. There was a lot of arguing and fighting between Angel's mother and stepfather. Eventually, they stopped getting along, and soon after, he left to be with his mistress and their child. Soon after, Angel's mother started to date again and found a man who could have changed Angel's and her family's entire lives.

A New Savior

Cheryl later met a man whom Angel referred to as their hero. His name was Dan. Dan came into their lives and immediately stepped up to take care of their family. He became their savior. He would fill their refrigerator with food, and make sure that the bills were paid. It was obvious to Angel that Dan liked her mom and all of her children. He treated all of them very well. Dan was a wealthy man, so he offered to take Cheryl and her children out of poverty. He offered her the dream of a big home with a white picket fence. Who wouldn't be intrigued by a man willing to give you and your children the world? Believe it or not, mom declined his offer. She had two reasons: One was that she was not into Caucasian guys, and the other reason was that she was still in love with John even though John had destroyed her heart, left her and her children for another woman, moved his mistress to a state where his wife and her children resided, and left them in poverty. John eventually found out about Dan and went into a rage. Angel watched her mom get out of a cab with Dan, while John, after being gone for two weeks, pulled up behind them in a separate vehicle. Soon afterward, a physical fight ensued where John grabbed Angel's mother and swung her to the ground while yelling and screaming. Although Dan attempted to help, Cheryl begged him to stay out of it. After the fight, Angel never saw

Dan again. What could have been a great life was suddenly flushed down the drain. Angel knew that her mother's actions were wrong and selfish. Why would she mess up a perfectly good relationship to go back to a man who didn't value her? Unfortunately, Cheryl was the only example of a true role model that would later be revealed through all of the failed relationships that Angel had.

The life they were living in Dallas was clearly unstable and the housing was inhabitable, so mom sent Angel and her siblings back to her father's house to live with him until she got back on her feet. Although they were older now, Bianca, their stepmother, dreaded the idea of them being back in the home, just as they had dreaded being back there. This was evident in her cold and dismissive treatment of them. She wasn't shy about voicing to Angel's father how she felt about them being there, and sadly enough, he allowed her behavior. Angel's father never fought for them or intervened when Bianca treated them badly. Angel didn't want to experience those feelings of rejection again, so she knew in her heart that she would not be there long. Cheryl did what she needed to do to quickly get her children back into a safe home.

Years later, Angel would realize that she needed to heal, she needed a genuine apology from her stepmother. Initially, Angel didn't want that apology because she felt as if Bianca knew her behavior was wrong, but she just didn't care. But still, God convinced Angel to let it all go, which she eventually did. Still, there was a part of her that found it so hard to let it go and truly forgive her stepmother.

It was during those later years, that Angel would reach out to her stepmom to try and obtain Annette's contact information. Remember, Annette was Bianca's best friend who took pity on Angel and her siblings and would care for them whenever they were visiting Angel's father's home. Angel wanted to keep a relationship with Annette and Bianca was the only person who could help her to do that.

Although Bianca was initially unwilling to give out the details of her best friend's whereabouts to Angel, she would eventually gives in after much discussion. Annette needed to know how much she was appreciated by Angel. Angel wanted to thank her for everything she had done. Contacting Annette was vital to Angel's healing. She was there for them when they all yearned for love, care, and attention when they did not receive it from the people who should have given it.

Islam

Angel still wondered what her father's thoughts were during this time. His actions spoke loudly as if he didn't care about them or their pain. And what about his religion and the responsibility of being a man of character that the Islam religion upholds? Her father's neglect and abandonment were the antitheses to what she had learned over the years growing up Muslim.

Angel didn't have a choice on what religion she wanted to be a part of. She was born into the Islamic faith, and that is what would be accepted and respected. Angel would later realize that despite the talk of how Muslim men and women should behave, her father or stepmother did not fit the description of God's (Allah's) standards or morals. To top it off, her father was an Imam—a leader in the Islamic community who couldn't be questioned. Talk about hypocrisy! Angel couldn't fathom how all she had faced while growing up could have happened within a Muslim community.

Angel got older, her Islamic faith faded; she distanced herself from the Islamic faith because of the many disappointments she experienced from her father's and stepmother's behavior. According to the Quran, not taking care of his wife and kids was not how Muslims were to behave—not something that Allah would approve of. The Quran teaches us to have faith in Allah (God); that family is the heart of the Muslim community, and that family is the most important influence on a child's life. After all, those children are to depend on their parents to protect and provide for them. It was traditional to pray to Allah five times a day, so as a Muslim leader, Angel often wondered to whom her father prayed. And what was he praying about? It sure couldn't have been about keeping his family protected or loved. When he was in the home as a husband and a father to Angel and the rest of the family, he was teaching from the Quran while on the podium at the Mosque every Friday, but once he left those doors, he was a completely different man- a lost, unhealed, broken man with no regard for family or the Islamic faith.

Knowing that her father was living his life in hypocrisy made Angel believe that all Muslim men were doing the same, so dating a Muslim man was definitely out of the question. Angel resented her father because of his behavior. Consequently, she also resented his Islamic religion and its teachings for years. Her father's actions caused her to rebel against it and everything it stood for. Eventually, Angel would find her way right back into the grips of a religion that she knew so little about despite what she had observed from her father. Angel realized that she couldn't blame an entire religion for her father's actions against his own family. Time and maturity helped her to understand that religion does not define who you are or who you will be, but for Angel, spirituality-building a healthy, loving connection to God is what would count the most.

Chapter Three

Dad's Death and The Void That Ensued

At age 18, Angel received the news that her father had passed away. She was in college and pregnant with her first child, a son, when she heard that her father was murdered. He was shot in the head after cashing a check at a check cashing store. Refusing to give up the money, he fought off his offenders and ended up losing his life. Angel's dad was known to be a tightwad with his money and didn't enjoy giving it away let alone allowing someone to take it from him. ironically, he died the same way he lived—

resistant. he was always very frugal and refused to give up any of his money to help financially support Angel and her siblings. He left their mother to fend for herself with five kids, and that pissed her off. Angel had no more tears left to shed for this man. She felt somewhat disconnected from the emotions of it all when she heard about his death. His death did not change Angel's feelings of resentment and abandonment. His heart had no love for her, and so in her mind, it was natural that she returned the favor.

Angel was now an adult, and she had had lots of time to get over her feelings of resentment toward her father, right? Only she hadn't. She couldn't believe that she didn't drop a tear at her father's funeral. Angel found herself attempting to express some empathy or feelings of sadness at her father's funeral, but couldn't squeeze out a tear for the sake of everyone else who was there, and who may question why she wasn't crying. Her heart had already hardened. She just couldn't shed another tear for a man that she barely knew. She was still angry at him, and she didn't want to let that feeling go. It's not that he deserved to die, because he didn't. He just didn't deserve her tears in his death. She had cried enough while he was living, so she thought that she had finally come to peace with the fact that her father had abandoned her. She had become numb to the man whom she had known to be her father. Before he was murdered and his body was in the grave, Angel's father was already gone from her heart.

Her father, her supposed protector, became the root of most of Angel's hurt, anger, and pain for many years before and after his death. Angel suppressed a lot of these negative feelings thinking that they would just go away. But they didn't.

Angel didn't understand what trauma was in her childhood, but in adulthood, she finally realized what it was. And in doing so, she began to learn how to accept her father for who he was. He was a man who chose a repeating cycle of lack—lack of love, lack of time, and lack of emotion. He too was unseen, unheard, and left with a broken heart. And he had done the same for his children. Angel had finally realized that her father only did what he knew how to do because that was what was shown and taught to him in his childhood. Angel's mother and father abandoned him as a young child, and he had to learn how to survive on his own while taking care of his siblings as a teenager he didn't know how to give love because he never experienced love for himself. Angel realized that she and her siblings had been living with his traumas throughout their entire childhood. Ignorance of their trauma had somehow become a blessing to them when they were growing up because they were oblivious to it. But as adults, they had grown into understanding, and their anger from their parent's divorce, their father's absence, and unstable home, unfortunately, came out in many ways through her promiscuity, poor choices, abusive and failed relationships, and troubled friendships. Some of Angel's siblings still refused to acknowledge the fact that their father's behavior affected their lives, and it still is affecting their lives. This is especially true for Angel and her sisters in how they perceive themselves now as women who are worthy to be loved. In adulthood, Angel experienced a lack of trust and confusion regarding her past trauma. She did not know how to feel or respond to men or relationships. The only feelings that are familiar to her are those of hurt, pain, resentment, and abandonment.

After Angel's father passed away, the feelings of hurt, pain, and abandonment didn't stop for many years. She blamed her father for that constant hurt. How could she know real love from a man or know how to give it? Her father's death caused Angel's open wounds to only go deeper and to fester. Angel wanted to be loved but her anger would eventually cause her to make choices with men that only resulted in her wound becoming deeper and more painful. Gregory Lang once said, "A daughter needs a dad to be the

30

standard against which she will judge men." This would be the constant void in Angel's life for many years.

As Angel looked around at everyone at her father's funeral, all she could see was a place filled with people who loved her father, who cried for her father, and who wished that he was still alive. She could not relate to these people; she felt nothing. It was as if her father was a stranger to her and these faces were strangers to her as well. Angel and her siblings stood cold and stone-faced; not a tear flowing. All they could do was stare at a casket that had the body of a man whom they once knew to be their father. Is it strange to not have feelings for a parent who has passed away? Who doesn't feel or have emotions when their father dies? The truth is Angel's father was a stranger to her who had shattered the heart of his children, and also the heart of his ex-wife Cheryl. He never apologized for all the hurt and pain that he caused them.

The strange faces at the funeral were relatives of her father whom Angel had never met or been introduced to. This was a part of her father's life that she did not know. It was like adding insult to injury since none of these people even knew of Angel and her siblings. The only thought Angel had was "why didn't they want to know us?" "How could they abandon their blood?" Even in his death, Angel's father

31

had failed them just as when he lived. Willie's new wife did not attempt to reconcile with Angel and her siblings; to this new family and extended relatives these people were strangers to Angel, and she was a stranger to them. In Angel's mind, all of this responsibility fell on her father to make it right and put things in order when he was alive. But he made no effort then, and he certainly couldn't do it now. Angel remembered a time when her father told her mother that he knew his children hated him and wished that he could have done better. He told their mother this shortly before he died as if he knew death was imminent for him. So many years had passed since their divorce, yet he waited until that moment to be honest. Why did he have to wait so many years before saying those words?

Angel's father didn't protect his children; he was a selfish liar. Angel remembered after the funeral that when she was around eight years old her father told her that in the event of his death, he had taken out an insurance policy to ensure that his children would be well taken care of. Angel didn't understand what he was saying at the time, but she never forgot those words. She found out upon his death that those words turned out to be a complete lie. He left Angel and her siblings with absolutely nothing--financially destitute. Everything that her father owned and had in his bank accounts and life insurance policy went to his wife Bianca and

Angel's half-siblings. Again, even in death, her father had failed them. It was a difficult pill to swallow.

After the funeral, Angel's stepmom decided to sell her father's car repair and dealership business and she never even offered a dime of the profits to Angel or her siblings. She kept it all for herself. Then, not even a year later, she was married to another Muslim man.

Speak to My Healing

Chapter Four

A TROUBLED HEART

You don't know people or can tell who they are until you have lived with them. Before Angel's father died, Angel and her siblings experienced more childhood trauma. Angel's Aunt Evelyn was one of her mother's brother's wife. As a child Angel didn't spend much time around her, but she knew who her aunt was. She knew her to be a very nice lady, and that was all she knew about her. However, that changed when Angel's mom decided to send them to spend the summer with their aunt Evelyn because going to their father's home was no longer an option; this is where Angel's next nightmare began.

While Angel and her siblings were visiting at their Aunt Evelyn's home, their mother would send her food stamps to ensure that Angel and her siblings never were without food. Angel never knew that her mom was sending food stamps for them because there was barely any food for them to eat at their aunt's home. Angel remembers walking several blocks with her siblings and her other kids who were in the home to the Salvation Army to get food, which became a daily ritual for them. They were so young at the time that she can't even recollect how they knew to find a Salvation Army and get food. Angel believes that God guided their footsteps there. Angel's aunt had four kids, and on top of that, she took in several other children from foster care. The children would walk with Angel and her siblings to the Salvation Army to eat every morning. Sadly enough, her aunt was never home so all of the kids had to take care of themselves. Angel will never forget the times that they would eat breakfast at her aunt's house: she would have to eat two types of cereal, Kix or Kaboom, and this was only on special occasions. They were only allowed to eat 7 to 8 pieces of cereal each since at least 13 kids were living in the home.

Angel remembers fighting with her aunt's foster kids every day over everything, including food. Aunt Evelyn was never around to see or stop the fights, so Angel and her siblings would always have to fend for themselves. She felt as if she were living in a foster care home herself and not actually with family. Angel found out later that she and her siblings never had food because their aunt was selling the food stamps her mother had sent them for drugs. Angel would hear her aunt laughing on the phone with her mom while telling her that everything was OK with them and that they were happy. Of course, Angel knew her aunt was lying. Truthfully, their aunt Evelyn didn't communicate with any of them, so she wouldn't have known if they were OK or happy. They were invisible to her. For any child, it would have been a terrible experience, but the worst part is that Angel's mom never believed that their aunt would have treated them that badly since their aunt was very good at covering up the truth. She was a functioning drug addict at best. Finally, Angel had a chance to tell her mother everything about all the horrific events that had taken place at her aunt's house. This led to a confrontation between her mother and her aunt. Even though Angel's aunt denied everything, Cheryl believed Angel and decided to bring her and her siblings back home. She canceled their aunt Evelyn out of their lives for years.

Many years later, somehow Evelyn wiggled her way back into Cheryl's life again. Angel's mom was always so forgiving; she allowed their aunt back into her life, and the two women became close again. Angel saw this as a betrayal, and it only brought up her full memories of the time Angel spent at her aunt's house. She felt as if her mom had no regard for her feelings and the trauma that her aunt had caused.

Older Men

Angel was very mature for her age and wasn't interested in guys her age. She was 13 years old at the time, and he was 19. Her family had just moved to Memphis, TN., and he was the first cute guy that she had noticed. Angel wasn't interested in dating him because she was too young to date, but that didn't stop her from noticing him. So, who was this mystery man? His name was Antoine and he lived in the same apartment complex as Angel and her family. A little rough around the edges, Antoine was the "bad boy" type. This "bad boy" behavior was attractive to Angel. Antoine was always getting into fights and threatening people around the neighborhood with a gun, so he was labeled as a bad boy. Everyone in the neighborhood feared him, but Angel was intrigued by that; it made her want to know more about him. Eventually, they ended up spending more and more time together to her mother's dismay. They only ever kissed and never had sex. Angel was a virgin and wanted to keep it that way until she was ready. Antoine never pressured Angel to do anything that she didn't want to do and that made her even more attracted to him because she saw that as kindness.

Antoine was caring, affectionate, and very protective of Angel. He was everything that Angel's father wasn't—he was loving to her and took care of her every need. He even taught Angel how to drive. But there was another side to Antoine... a dark side. He was extremely jealous and didn't like to see other guys around Angel even though he had a girlfriend at the time. If he saw another man in Angel's presence, he would scare them off by threatening violence. One day, Angel went to a club with a fake ID and an hour later, Antoine stormed through the crowd of people looking for her. As soon as Angel saw the anger and rage on his face she immediately ran out of the club and hid from him for almost a week.

Shortly after that time, Angel felt safe enough to venture out of her home and walk to her best friend's house. However, that walk would take her past Antoine's apartment. Angel remembers seeing Antoine sitting on the stairs with his friends. She conjured up enough courage to keep walking and not show him the fear on her face. She finally locked eyes with Antoine and saw daggers in his eyes. His piercing stare went directly to her heart. Angel tried to walk as fast as possible past Antoine's apartment, but his stare turned suddenly into a deviant smile and that's when Angel heard someone quickly running up behind her. Then, Boom! Angel was knocked onto the ground face-first. Seeing her in pain gave Antoine the satisfaction that he needed. It all happened so fast that she never saw it coming. Once Angel was able to get up, she heard Antoine yell across the field, that's what you get! All his friends laughed. This infuriated Angel, so she managed to find a bat and headed towards Antoine's car and begin busting out all of his car windows yelling, "And this is what you get!"

At this point, Angel felt no sense of fear even though she knew how crazy Antoine was. As he continued to yell at her, she stared at him with a smirk on her face. Suddenly, Antoine pulled out his gun, walked up to her, and place the gun against her temple. As Angel turn slightly to look at Antoine, she realized she was staring into the face of a demon. She said, "If you're going to kill me, then you can kill me as I walk away from you, coward." Even at such a young age, Angel knew she had to show strength even if underneath she was shaking in fear, she could not let Antoine know that he had any power over her. It was then that Angel turned her back towards Antoine and began walking away. As she waited for the gun to go off, someone had gone to find Angel's mother and she came running out screaming and crying, begging Antoine to spare her daughter's life. The entire neighborhood watched as this surreal moment played out. Still, Angel had no fear because she knew that God had her back. Angel was able to walk away that day with her life, but she hadn't learned a valuable lesson about men-True love doesn't exist.

Shortly thereafter her relationship with Antoine ended, and Angel got involved with another older man, which led to another toxic relationship.

Speak to My Healing

Chapter Five

TAKE CARE OF ME

At 16, Angel began dating another older man who was 24 years of age. It seemed as if these older men that Angel got involved with were just convenient fillers of the void left by her father's absence. This new older man's name was Phil. Phil was her next-door neighbor and he was also a drug dealer. Again, Angel was mesmerized by the glitz and glamour of the nice things that Phil was able to buy and flaunt throughout the neighborhood. Angel and her family didn't have much money, and money was what always caught her attention. Phil was tall, dark, and handsome—just her type.

The thing is that Phil had a girlfriend, so Angel considered him off-limits at first and didn't pursue him. Eventually, Phil was the one who approached Angel and began giving her money every day and buying her new clothes and new shoes. Angel never questioned why he did any of these things, she just enjoyed them. Angel knew that she was tired of going to school with raggedy clothes and shoes, so she was thankful for anything that Phil gave her.

Angel felt that she could finally fit in with all of her classmates in high school with the new clothes and shoes that Phil's money provided. Angel loved that Phil took care of her, even giving her money to help her mom pay the bills and buy food for her and her siblings. Phil was such a generous man, but his generosity begged the question: why would a grown man be interested in a 16-year-old girl? The conversations between Angel and Phil started to become more and more intense to the point that he began to neglect his girlfriend because he was spending so much time with Angel. Phil's attention toward Angel became more and more intense as well. Of course, his girlfriend became angry once she found out about Angel, but Phil didn't seem to care. Eventually, Phil and Angel engaged in sexual intercourse. It was Angel's first time, and she became pregnant. When Angel found out she was pregnant, she was scared and also devastated. Phil assured her that he would be there for her and the baby every step of the way, but that didn't alleviate Angel's fears. She didn't want to be a mother at 16 years old; she was still a kid herself.

Eight weeks into her pregnancy, Angel, unfortunately, suffered a miscarriage. She figured that maybe God knew that she wasn't ready for the hardship of being a young mom. Even after the miscarriage, Phil and Angel continued to be intimate. Now, at the time, Phil still had girlfriends who were in and out of his life, but they were all of age. Yet, he was still keeping up his relationship with this teenage girl, Angel. His current girlfriend always hated Angel because she knew something was going on between Angel and Phil and knew that they weren't just friends. Phil never tried to hide his friendship with Angel, so there wasn't anything any of his girlfriends could do about it. He never admitted to having sex with Angel, but I'm sure they knew, and so did her mom.

Any girlfriends that Phil had accepted his behavior because he had money and he always took care of his women. His girlfriends often questioned him, but he would get really upset and defend his relationship with Angel by telling them that Angel was only his neighbor.

Everyone else in the neighborhood knew what was going on. Their entire relationship could be described as very weird. Even Angel's mom was aware of their relationship, which was quite unusual for a mother to condone a 16-year-old girl being with a 24-year-old man. There was a part of Angel that wanted her mom to say something and maybe end the relationship because it would mean that she was at least paying attention to Angel. As a mom, Angel expected her to be angry and say something to the both of them about their relationship, but because Phil was taking care of them financially, her mom turned a blind eye because she was reaping the benefits of their relationship. Angel dated Phil until she was 25 years old. He continued to always be there for her financially and even though he had other girlfriends, if Angel needed him, Phil would immediately drop everything to take care of her. Phil was the first man to step into the role that Angel's father should have, and Angel's main attraction to Phil was a financial one. Angel learned many lessons from Phil on how a man should take care of women. Although Angel dated guys within her age range from her high school, it wasn't the same as dating older men because the younger guys were not financially capable of taking care of her. They didn't have enough money to finance Angel's life and lifestyle. She considered the younger guys she dated as a fun distraction. But when Angel needed money, she had no choice but to look at dating someone older, someone like Phil.

High School Refuge

The school was always a place for Angel to hide away from her neighborhood and her home life. It became her home away from home. Angel had many friends in high school who helped her get through life's struggles, like when her lights were cut off every other month at home. After moving from Dallas to Memphis, Angel's mother decided to rekindle her marriage with John. During hard times, John-Angel's stepfather would steal the electricity from their next-door neighbor by attaching an extension cord to the neighbor's electricity box located outside. At times, Cheryl would wait on John to bring food home, which often consisted of five dollars worth of bologna. There were other times that Angel and her siblings would fry fat to eat, or Angel and her mother would walk for miles to pick up groceries from a church. Angel and her siblings hated the fact that their mother depended so much on a man and made very little effort to make things happen on her own. Angel had no respect for her stepfather and thought her mother could do so much better than a loser like him. Eventually, her stepfather couldn't handle the responsibilities of being a husband and a stepfather and started smoking crack cocaine. After finding this out, Cheryl had to put him out of the house permanently.

Angel could always rely on her friends to be there for her. When the heat went out in her house and they had to use a heated furnace to stay warm, Angel's friends would spend the night with her as if nothing was happening. They all slept on a pallet where they would pile dirty clothes on the floor and cover the clothes with a large blanket to form the illusion of a bed. Angel could depend on her friends to be by her side without judgment.

Eventually, other guys came into Angel's life. While in high school, she met a guy named Stan who was a 19-year-old drug dealer and high school dropout. Angel was so intrigued by him—his gold teeth, his jewelry, and his nice car. Stan was a ladies' man. All of the girls in high school liked him. He didn't attend school, but he would hang around there looking for younger girls to date. Angel would walk home from school some days with a group of friends, and he would drive up beside them. This was when he first noticed Angel and pointed her out. Angel was shocked because she never considered herself the pretty girl of the group. Most of her friends were light-skinned with long hair, which was considered the image of beauty, but Angel was a darker complexion, was tall, and skinny, and she didn't see herself as pretty as her friends. Yet, Stan wanted her. Her father never told Angel that she was pretty so every compliment that came from any guy was valuable to her. Eventually, Angel started dating Stan-which made a couple of her friends upset. It's what's called "the light-skinned syndrome"-when light-skinned girls feel superior and privileged over dark-skinned girls. During her high school years, it wasn't boys whom Angel wanted to spend her time chasing. She was more interested in maintaining a certain way of life and making sure she had money, and older men with money were her way to obtaining that.

Angel had a close friend named Shayla. Shayla was what Angel called a hustler. She never knew how Shayla was able to dress so nicely and she always seemed to have money. Turns out, Shayla was a booster who would pop tags off of high-end clothing stores in the mall and she was a master at it. Angel eventually joined her in this venture because it was a means of survival for her.

Alongside her boyfriends who would spend money on her and buy her things, Angel now had another means of getting her the nice clothes and jewelry she wanted to show off. She got very experienced in stealing clothes. She would calmly walk out of the store with the stolen clothes in the store's shopping bags that she and Shayla would grab from behind the store counter. After doing this for a couple of years, Angel and Shayla eventually got caught. They didn't serve any jail time, luckily, but the money that had to be spent on an attorney was not worth all the shoplifting they had done. After standing before a judge who told Angel that she could face up to a year for the crime, Angel never stole out of a mall or anywhere else again in her life. Angel kept dating Stan for about six months until she found out that he began dating another girl who went to the same high school. Angel overheard this girl telling her friends that she met a guy named Stan and she described him exactly, even describing his car. Every time Angel would see this girl she would hear her bragging about Stan, and she would even wear a chain around her neck that spelled out his name. Angel was hurt, devastated, and angry. She knew that Stan was playing her on purpose, so one day she saw him at a club and once the night ended, she went out to his car to wait for him. Angel was always ready for a fight and would put herself in compromising situations. She got into a physical fight with Stan's newfound girlfriend that night where she jumped on top of Stan's car and began stomping on the hood to try to destroy it. Once she damaged the car, she jumped down to begin punching the new girlfriend with all of the anger and rage that she had inside of her. Her ride-or-die friend- Shayla pointed a gun to threaten anyone who dared to jump into the fight. That was the last night of their relationship.

Chapter Six

A FIGHT FOR HER LIFE

Angel's dream was always to go to college. She dreamt of going to Howard University to pursue a degree in criminal justice, but her plans got altered when she became pregnant after high school. But being pregnant didn't stop Angel from going to college. She had every intention of fulfilling her dream so she applied for college within her area with the hopes of improving her and her child's life. At age 18 she was pregnant and scared. The baby's father, Dewayne lived in the projects and was a street corner hustler. He was a very handsome guy who ran the streets a lot and had no direction. Of course, his looks weren't going to help Angel take care of her baby unless he became a gigolo. DeWayne's mom had kicked him out when he was 16, so he stayed with friends and other family members from time to time. Angel doubted if she and Dewayne were making the right decision to bring a child into the world. Before Angel found out she was pregnant, she and DeWayne got into a physical altercation because he found out that Angel was still dating her ex-boyfriend-Pete.

During a physical fight with De-Wayne, one of his friends went behind Angel and tripped her, which caused her to fall to the ground. While she was on the ground, DeWayne hit her in the head with a brick. Blood was everywhere, but Angel didn't notice that she was bleeding when she got back up. Her adrenaline was pumping from anger. Despite her injuries, Angel was ready to continue the fight, so she ripped off a tree branch that was nearby and began chasing DeWayne with it. At the same time, Angel didn't notice that an ambulance was chasing her down the street to help her. Eventually, she was placed into the ambulance and taken to the hospital. The blunt force of the brick had caused her to go in and out of consciousness.

Angel's injury required her to get 36 stitches in her head. Just two days later, Angel was back on the streets with a swollen face and a smile. Angel's mom was horrified and extremely upset about what DeWayne had done to her. Her mother encouraged her to call the police, but Angel didn't want to do it. She didn't want to have the police in her business. But her mom insisted so she had no choice but to report it. DeWayne was charged with aggravated assault and was arrested. As his case was ongoing, that was when Angel discovered that she was pregnant with her son. When Dewayne found out, he was so happy and hoped that Angel would drop the charges so that he could be a part of his son's life. Angel did drop the charges, but unfortunately, the state picked his case back up. DeWayne was sentenced to two years in jail. Before his sentencing, he was able to spend every day with Angel while she was pregnant. He was so gracious to her—treating her like a queen and tending to every need. Fortunately, DeWayne was able to be there for his son's birth. At least he had a chance to spend a little time with his son before he went to jail.

Upon DeWayne's release from jail, he turned his life around. With Angel's help, he received his GED and landed a job with a roofing company. Angel helped him to get his GED because she wanted him to be a better role model for his son. She knew her son needed a father in his life and Angel was proud of DeWayne for wanting to change his life around.

One day, Angel received a phone call from Dewayne's best friend who worked with him at the same job site for the roofing company. On the phone DeWayne's best friend kept repeating the words, "He's gone; he's dead!" Angel thought he was crazy—what could he be saying? She didn't want to believe that he was telling her that DeWayne, the father of her son was dead. When Angel finally realized what he was saying, she then asked him how? "He fell through a hole in the roof and fell 30 feet," he said.

The irony of this is that DeWayne and Angel had gotten into a huge argument the night before and she told him that he would never see his son again. Angel didn't mean it when she said those words. She never thought that DeWayne would die the very next day. Since then, Angel has believed that there is power in the tongue. she will never forget those words and has felt the guilt of it ever since. Despite all of the struggles they had in their relationship and the times in the past when DeWayne treated Angel terribly, he didn't deserve to die. The best thing DeWayne did for Angel was to leave her with the gift of their son.

When their son was born and as he grew, he reminded Angel so much of DeWayne—his looks and his mannerisms all were just like his father's. Angel still often wishes that DeWayne were alive to see his son.

When Angel was 19 years old and in her second year at college, she was having the best time of her life. College life was exciting! She attended an HBCU and was taken in as a Sigma sweetheart- seems like moments after she stepped on campus. Soon afterward, Angel decided to pledge to Zeta Phi Beta Sorority, Inc. She was president of the Pan Hellenic Council two years in a row. She was involved in all of the step shows and went to all of the parties, and she loved it! Her Fraternity brothers, Phi Beta Sigma, Inc were like her blood brothers, and they were very protective, loving, and caring. Angel had everything that she wanted and needed.

One particular time, there was a party that Angel planned to attend, and she always depended on one of her Frat brothers or Sorors to pick her up. There was an agreement that one of my fraternity brothers would pick her up to attend the party, but after several hours of waiting on him to arrive at her home, she received a phone call saying that he was too intoxicated to drive and that they would send someone else to pick up Angel. Angel trusted her Frat brothers, so she was okay with the decision. The guy who showed up was someone she had never seen before. He was of tan complexion, very tall-about 6'5 in height, with a huge body frame, friendly, and well-mannered. He met Angel's mother because she never left with a stranger without taking a picture of their car tags and sending it to a family member or introducing them to a family member just in case something happened. Before leaving out the door, the stranger shook her mother's hand, smiled, and they left.

The rest of the night resulted in Angel being sexually assaulted by this guy. It was brutal and traumatizing. Before being raped, she was first taken to the stranger's mother's house, where she met his mother and other family members. There was a celebration of some kind that day, so everyone in the house appeared to be happy. Despite being in a happy environment, it was not Angel's destination, and she did not agree to this curb ball on the way to the party. She had asked "what time are we leaving?" and his response was, "soon". "Soon had turned into an hour, and once she and the stranger left, the face of what was laughing and smiling at his mother's house, turned into the face of a demonic spirit. Angel felt that something was wrong and that she was in immediate danger. Once inside the vehicle, the stranger began to yell at Angel and threatened to kill her. She would never forget those haunting words, "You're going to die tonight". The stranger then began driving Angel around a graveyard site where he told her that there is where she would be buried. After circling the gravesite for thirty minutes, the stranger then proceeded to drive towards what would look like an abandoned home. The stranger forced Angel out of the car, opened the front door without a key, and grabbed her by her arm. The house was gloomy and empty except for a dusty mattress and dirty blankets. There is no doubt that this man had raped women here before. Angel was not the type of woman who would beg for her life. She knew that God would protect her and that he would not leave her side. There was a calmness about her. Although she was afraid for her life, she refused to show this stranger her fear. Angel was raped that night in an abandoned house located in South Memphis on a filthy mattress. As she was being raped, her only thoughts were, "God help me out of this", and He did just that. She mustered up enough courage to challenge her rapist and convinced him to let her go by telling this stranger that he didn't have to continue to rape her, or for that matter, kill her. She used reverse psychology by telling him that she loved him and that she would marry him. Strangely enough, the attacker believed her and began to cry like a baby. He said, "Do you mean that?" Angel replied, "yes, I do. I love you". Afterward, the stranger instructed Angel to go to the car so that he could take her home. Angel was relieved but continued to pray that she would make it home. To Angel, getting home was the longest ride of her life! On the way there, Angel and the stranger would ride by two police cars and Angel contemplated jumping out of the car. She weighed her options of trusting her attacker to get her back home safely or risking this 6'5 300 lb. man killing her before she had even gotten a chance to unlock her door to jump out of the car to run towards the police for help. She would hear the voice of God instructing her to calmly remain in the vehicle, and that she would live to see another day. After being dropped off at her home, Angel ran into the arms of her mother where she cried and cried while telling her mother that she had been raped by the very same man that had shaken her mother's hand. That night, Angel went to the hospital to have a rape kit performed, but once she returned home, she would rock herself to sleep for comfort. Her trust, once again, had been broken by a man.

The police were also called that night. As Angel explained to the police what happened, it was as if she was living in a nightmare. Her voice trembled as she spoke about the events that led up to her being raped. The police took a report, and several days later, her attacker was arrested. The court date was set, and Angel, once again, would have to muster up enough courage to face her attacker. As she listened to the judge speak highly of the man who raped her, she was in disbelief. It was in court that Angel learned that her rapist was a Marine Corps veteran and a Masonic member. Most high-powered men such as judges, attorneys police officers, and politicians are Masons; therefore, there is a brotherhood attached to this devil. Because of her attacker's affiliation with Masons, the case against him was dismissed based upon his word of it being consensual sex; he had no consequences to pay. Angel was sick to her stomach. Unfortunately, many men get away with violating women and children because of male judges who see women and children as nothing more than "objects" that need to be used and abused based on their needs. Rapists and child molesters are often given light sentences or no sentences at all since many judges who are men are thinking with their sick, sexually deviant minds where they justify their mental illness. In their minds, when a woman has been raped, it's "so what's the problem?" or "Just get over it". The problem is that she didn't ask to be raped, and she surely didn't consent to have sex with this man. Women are NOT a man's property, and women/children should never be inappropriately touched. Kudos to the judicial system for failing yet another woman.

Being raped affected not only the relationships that Angel had with men but also their relationship with her son. Angel was angry and she would direct her anger to the men in her life. Her anger would cause her to abuse men emotionally and mentally by emasculating them when she would see signs of failures that reflected that of her father. Then, she would abandon relationships first for fear of being abandoned by the men.

It was difficult for Angel to establish a relationship with her son early on after the rape because it made her feel dirty when her son would kiss, hug, or touch her. Angel would question any sign of affection when it came to males.

Chapter Seven

LIFE AS A SINGLE MOM

Eventually, Angel graduated from college and found herself as a single mother with two children out of wedlock. She had to find a steady job to take care of her children because she wanted to be the best mom she could be for them. However, jobs were scarce even though Angel had a Bachelor's degree. The next best thing to do was to do something that she was good at and to make money doing it. She began doing her hair. Angel had learned to braid hair when she was only seven years old, so she figured she would use that talent now to braid hair and do so out of her home. She was a natural at it and made much money doing it. It was the perfect situation working from home because Angel got to take her kids to school and pick them up, knowing they would always be safe. Working from home was a true blessing for Angel and her kids. She didn't miss having a 9-to-5 job that would take her away from spending time nurturing her kid's needs to create the bond that needed to happen between a mother and their child.

Angel became pregnant with her second child, a daughter when she was 20 years old, and DeWayne was not the father. There was someone that Angel dated before she started dating DeWayne. His name was Pete, and he was a street guy who also lived in the projects. He was a drug dealer as well.

Angel's pregnancy sort of came as a payback to Dewayne. She got pregnant with Pete's baby shortly after she and Dewayne broke up. And the worst part was that DeWayne and Pete were friends, but Angel didn't know this until she and Dewayne became serious about their relationship. Angel never intended to get pregnant with Pete's child. It turns out that during sex, Pete had taken the condom off and Angel never knew. Of course, she was upset about what Pete had done, and she was even more upset when she found out that he and Dewayne were good friends and that she was now pregnant with Pete's child.

Angel wanted to ensure that her children's fathers were a part of their lives, so one day when her daughter was just a year old, Angel agreed to let Pete keep her for the weekend. When Angel got her daughter back, she came back to her drunk. Angel found out that Pete and his mother had given her baby beer in her baby bottle instead of milk. From that point on she never allowed him to keep her daughter again. Why was she always ending up in these situations with these terrible men?

As years went by, Pete did everything he could do to earn Angel's trust back with him after the beer incident. And yet again, Angel allowed him back into her life. This was a huge mistake. One day, he asked Angel to pick him up around 1:00 AM. She would end up picking him up from a drug dealing area. Unbeknownst to Angel, Pete had drugs on him. Angel knew that Pete sold drugs so there is a part of her that knew what she was getting into when she drove to pick him up. She asked Pete that night if he had any drugs on him and he told her he didn't. That lie, led both of them to jail that night.

One year later after this incident, Angel was still connected to Pete, and he was still a part of her life. She called him one day because she needed transportation for her kids. He agreed to help her and told her that he had an extra car that she could borrow. After driving the car for several months, Angel felt that something was off because there were temporary tags on the car that could not be renewed. Angel decided to use a black magic marker to artistically draw updated numbers on the temporary tags. Pete gave her lots of excuses as to why he could not get permanent tags for the car, but she didn't believe him. Angel asked an ex-boyfriend of hers who was a police officer to run the VIN on the car and it came back as a stolen car. Angel was in shock, so she planned to leave the car on the Interstate and called a friend to pick her up. Once her friend arrived, they both wiped down the car of Angel's fingerprints and left the scene. Angel didn't speak to Pete for two years after that. But she still didn't learn her lesson. After those two years, she connected with Pete again. This time, Pete convinced Angel to drive him and his friend to a bank because Pete said that their licenses were suspended, and they couldn't drive themselves there. Pete told Angel that he needed to withdraw some money and that he would give her money for their daughter. Unfortunately, she believed him. Little did Angel know that she would end up being the getaway driver for a bank robbery that Pete and his friend were committing. There was a voice in Angel's head that told her to look in her rearview mirror as Pete and his friend were running toward the vehicle with stacks of money in their hands, and some of the money flying everywhere. After noticing them with the money, Angel immediately put the car in drive and left them there. They deserved to go to jail. She felt she had seriously dodged a bullet that day. She had no idea that she was part of the getaway plan. After this incident, Angel truly believed that Pete was deliberately trying to send her to jail out of revenge for having a child with his friend DeWayne and dating him at the same time. Pete was vindictive! How evil could a person be?

Bad Choices

Angel knew that she was not making the best choices with men in her life. There was indeed a pattern of her gravitating to dysfunctional or broken men just like her mother did. And now she was having their babies. She didn't want to see her children end up making the same choices that she made in their relationships. She knew she had to change. She could no longer be a product of her choices.

Angel knew that the men she was dating were drug dealers and could go to jail at any time, but she was too greedy to listen to reason from anyone. She saw men as the source of financial survival, which is all they meant to her.

Although Angel's mom set an example of choosing bad men and having toxic relationships, she was a very good mom, just with many shortcomings. She taught Angel to be a strong woman and always made sure that her kids were loved, cared for, and nurtured to the best of her ability. And Angel wanted to do the same with her children.

Angel wanted a different path for her life and her children. She often wished that she could have done a better job of choosing men so that her children could have their fathers in their lives. Understandably, parenting doesn't come with a handbook, so Angel did the best that she could. Unknowingly, it was a repeat of what her mother had done to them as children, but only worse. She knew she had to do better.

But Angel truly believes that God has continued to guide her through these struggles so that she can be an inspiration to her children and others.

Chapter Eight

TIME TO GROW UP

Hell-Mate

After putting herself through so many toxic relationships, Angel met a guy named Victor. He was tall, dark, and handsome. He was extremely charming and definitely her type. He was the one that Angel's heart desired.

Victor was a troubled man who ran from relationship to relationship. He was a retired Navy veteran who had moved from Norfolk, Virginia to Memphis, TN. They met one day while Angel was driving down the street. She noticed this handsome man driving beside her while making funny faces and smiling. Eventually, Victor told Angel to pull over to the gas station. They talked for hours at the gas station and eventually exchanged numbers. He noticed that Angel didn't wear earrings, and a few days later, he purchased a pair and gifted them to her. Angel saw Victor twice before he disappeared into thin air. She was very disappointed and didn't understand why he disappeared. He stopped answering phone calls, and Angel didn't hear from him for years.

Angel would find out later that Victor was a married man. For two years, she did not know about his marriage. Victor was good at hiding things.

Although Angel heard many things from his previous marriage regarding his emotional and behavioral issues, Victor and Angel had a good relationship. She believed that she was special to him. Victor was a dysfunctional man and sneaky. Yet, Angel was still drawn to him enough to later marry him. She thought that he was her best friend and her soul mate. Victor didn't come from a stable home life, just like her father, both his mother, and father had abandoned him, so at the age of 17, he decided to join the military.

Victor was a womanizer and a manipulator, who often charmed his way into women's lives by marrying them and then leaving. Angel didn't think that she would become one of his victims, but she did. She thought things could have turned out differently with her. Falling for his lies repeatedly, she continued to forgive him, just as she had done with her father. Angel always fell for the guy with mommy or daddy issues, or maybe the reason was just her denial and belief that these men would change their ways for her. Angel began to realize more and more that she had a weakness for these types of men.

A couple of years later, Victor and Angel ran into each other again.

He explained to her that he was moving back to Virginia and that he needed to store his clothes at her home for a couple of days. Those couple of days somehow turned into seven months. After living with her for seven months, Angel came outside one early morning to find Victor's SUV written in bright red lipstick: "Call Your Wife". Angel was confused, so she asked him about it, and he admitted that he was married, but separated. He left that day, returning with more of his things, and then moved completely in.

Victor and Angel were like best friends. In the beginning, there was no intimacy, but he was very intelligent, so she loved the way that he stimulated her mind. He talked about everything from the Bible to Politics. He was well-versed, and Angel was intrigued. He filled a void in her heart and mind.

Victor taught Angel a lot, even how not to trust men. To Angel, Victor was the King of snakes, the King of Lies, and the King of Deceit. He was a wolf in sheep's clothing. He was a womanizer who was hurt by his mentally ill mother, and he wanted to inflict the same type of hurt and pain onto other women. Angel didn't realize how dysfunctional he was. His mother was schizophrenic, and he was abandoned by his father. Angel kept attracting men who were either abandoned by their mother or father (the same as her father). History was repeating itself.

Still, Victor and Angel eventually began to date, which led to a serious relationship. After dating for about a year and a half, she encouraged him to get a divorce because she refused to continue to be in a relationship with a married man. Angel was getting harassing phone calls from Victor's wife as if she was the one who destroyed their marriage, and she didn't like that. It made her feel guilty and ashamed of what she was doing. None of that mattered because, by this time, Angel was completely enraptured with this man. She loved him, but not enough to continue with this type of humiliation. He had to make a decision, and fast!

Unfortunately, Angel had to leave Victor before he decided to get his divorce. When he came back into her life, he had his divorce papers in hand. Angel was convinced that this man truly loved her until she met and spoke with one of his ex-wives. This is when she discovered that Victor had a pattern of getting into serious relationships while still married. This was not the most recent ex-wife, but the first wife (Diana) who decided to give Angel all the tea. She had known him since he was a teenager and knew his entire family history, What she told Angel about him was the opposite of what she was told by him and what she knew of this man to be. Angel didn't want to believe a word she said, but her instincts told her that this woman was telling the truth. She was very sweet, non-confrontational, and honest. Angel decided to keep her conversations in the back of her mind while she continued to move forward with Victor until she saw something different.

Victor introduced Angel to his ex-wife Diana, who lived in Virginia with two of his firstborn sons). She invited them to stay at her home, and while they were there, Angel had the time of her life. She had never met anyone like Diana. It was a blessing to have met her, even though Victor mostly negatively spoke about her. In speaking with her, Angel discovered more information about Victor that she couldn't believe. Victor was not even his real name; It was Lavell, and Lavelle had a different side to him that she would discover later on.

Diana also warned Angel that Victor had several other children and that some of them he refused to claim as his own because he was too embarrassed. Lavell (aka Victor) told Angel that he had 3 kids when they first met. It was more like 6, and then 6 turned into 9 kids.

After the fifth year, she began to fall more and more in love with Victor despite all of the deceit and lies. But as the years continued to pass, so did the love. Angel and Victor eventually married after being in a toxic relationship for 9 years where there was domestic violence and emotional abuse. Their marriage lasted 30 days. Victor eventually abandoned Angel just as her father had done her as a child.

After years of being disconnected, Victor came back into Angel's life. He received her number from Angel's sister while searching for her contact online. Angel learned that he had been searching for her for years. The chemistry that was there years before was still there. He was a type of love that could not be shaken. Angel was still in love with him, and he was in love with her. They were in a relationship that lasted nine years. The separation devastated Angel, and it took her six years to get over him. Unfortunately, the healing process button would have to reset after the reconnection.

The day that Angel heard from Victor was shocking. Victor never wanted the divorce he refused to sign the divorce papers, so the separation lingered for years while they each dated other people. There was joy in his voice when he told Angel that he had finally gotten her phone number. He told her he had been searching for her for a long time. Angel enjoyed hearing his soothing and familiar voice; she was excited even though she was a little angry at the same time because she felt that Victor had failed her as a man and as a husband. And after so many years passing by between them, Angel had no idea of who he was, where he lived, and how he had lived his life thus far. This man who was once her best friend had suddenly become a stranger to her.

Angel fell in love with who she thought was her soulmate, but in fact, he turned out to be fact her hell-mate.

Victor wasn't just another guy for Angel – not this time. She did love him even though it was such a toxic relationship. The culminating moment in their relationship that marked the end, was when Victor ended up getting stabbed by Angel because of his constant infidelities. After finding out that he was cheating with another woman after taking him back in, she couldn't take it anymore. The anger she felt toward him, and possibly all of the other men who had hurt her in her life reached its highest point and took control of her mind. She realized after she stabbed Victor that even though he did survive the stabbing she could have killed him. It was then that she realized that she needed to let him go.

Casino Life

The original plan when Angel attended college was to become an attorney and later a judge because she wanted to help people. But, after she graduated, things took a turn. Her dreams had gone left. She found herself being a single mother, and out of work. Braiding hair out of her home was no longer an option since she had developed tendonitis in her fingers and hand from hair braiding. Even with a degree in Political Science, she couldn't find a job or afford law school. Since Angel was out of work, she decided to work as a cocktail waitress at a casino in Tunica, MS.

Imagine going to school for 4 years, maintaining a 3.4 grade point average, graduate with a BA degree in Political Science with two small children only to be disappointed with not being able to find a good-paying job in your field or any field. This was another blow for Angel because all she wanted was to be better for herself and her children. Having a degree and landing a job as a cocktail waitress was super embarrassing and frustrating. This made Angel regret going to college. Four years of loans and scholarships were wasted!

Being hired as a cocktail waitress at a casino turned out not to be so bad after all. Angel made more money in tips than she would have made in salary with a college degree. Being a cocktail waitress came with the perks of wealthy men (including celebrities) who were willing to tip anywhere from $10-$100 per drink and if they were intoxicated, the money went up!

Cocktail waitresses wore enticing costumes that would manipulate or encourage the men to spend more money gambling while watching beautiful women walk by. The skirts or shorts would be super short, but cute, and they wore a bustier for tops so that their breasts would sit high and be the first to be noticed. The casinos were sexualized industry-especially for cocktail waitresses. Men would enjoy the looks of beautiful women with skimpy outfits. Of course, this increased a woman's tips. It wasn't unusual for a cocktail waitress to be tipped $100 for a bottle of water.

Most times, the men would ask the cocktail waitresses to become their "lucky charm" while they took their chances at the dice (craps) table or Blackjack table. Other gamblers perceived a cocktail waitress as a "black cat" jinx, so they preferred that they didn't come near them. The environment was full of excitement and full of entertainment.

The casinos probably will never admit this, but they were kind of racist with the black waitresses. At every casino, there were always more white than black waitresses. To get a job as a black cocktail waitress, you had to look a certain way so that every race of men would be attracted to you. Luckily for Angel, she fit the bill. Although she made a good amount of money, Angel didn't make half as much as the white waitresses did. She remembers a time when she was serving a wealthy gambler because he was in her section. She was happy that he was tipping me $20 per drink, but when it was time for Angel to be relieved for a break by a white waitress, she bragged that she was being tipped $100 a drink. Angel was so hurt but kept her feelings inside because she had finally realized that racism was real.

Angel only worked at the casino part-time. She worked the graveyard shift-12 am-8 am because she didn't want to wear out her welcome with her mother who often babysat for Angel. Angel's mother was the only one who stood by her side through thick and thin and the only person that she could ever trust with her children. Angel trusted her mother with some of her darkest secrets-which would later be revealed to her other siblings when her mother got angry with her.

Angel had learned the art of manipulating men to get what she wanted by cutting off her feelings, which wasn't very hard to do since being abandoned by her father). She didn't care about whether or not they had feelings for her or how much money they had decided to spend on her in one night. They meant nothing to Angel. There was an older guy that Angel met at the casino where she worked who added her as an authorized user on his unlimited American Express Card; bought her a car and always gave her money. He confessed to Angel's mother that he wanted to be in a relationship with her and wanted her help in convincing her to be with him. She laughed at the thought of being in a relationship with him because he was twice her age. Others would (during her work shift) ask her supervisor if they could pay them to allow her to leave work and fly out to Vegas that night on their private jet. She was often asked to be flown out on trips and would pay Angel's mother $500 to babysit for the weekend. Cheryl happily accepted the offer. Angel's mother allowed her to live her best life in her twenties while she babysat Angel's children when Angel wanted to get away, and in exchange, she was compensated with money, clothes, and expensive jewelry.

When it came to men (after many failed relationships), the only thing that made Angel happy was money and gifts. She stopped caring about love and affection. In short, she was damaged, and she needed healing.

Speak to My Healing

Chapter Nine

SPEAK TO MY HEALING

The Savior

Without a doubt, Angel was always the person to want to help people whether they were good or bad. In counseling, this is called the Carl Rogers "humanistic" theory approach in which all humans are considered to be potentially "good". She viewed all people to be good until they showed her otherwise, and even then, she would give them a second chance. Angel had a huge heart, and would often put others before herself, and that was why men and children were particularly attracted to Angel. Men perceived her love of helping people as a form of weakness or vulnerability. This made Angel an easy target. Children on the other hand are honest and pure. They can easily sense the evil and the good in people.

If Angel saw children wandering around in grocery stores or department stores without their parents, she would try to get to them before another stranger did and take them right to their parents. Angel would get angry and confront the parent for allowing their child to be susceptible to getting kidnapped, raped, or killed. She grew tired of seeing kids' faces on Walmart poster boards asking, "Have you Seen Me?" This came from Angel's loving, compassionate, nurturing, and caring heart.

Angel despised parents who neglected or abused their children; her next-door neighbor used to abuse her kids. She had about five or six of them. One particular night, Angel's neighbor put one of her daughters out on the porch. She was about 12 years old at the time, and it was a school night. Angel watched the young girl as she remained on the porch for several hours crying. Finally, at midnight, Angel had enough and told the girl to come inside her house. Angel allowed her to bathe, fed her, and let her sleep in one of her children's beds. The following morning, Angel dressed the young girl in her daughter's clothes and took her children and the little girl to school. After dropping them off at school the following morning, the little girl's mother knocked on Angel's door to ask if she had seen her daughter. Angel was so angry that she told her, "No!" and slammed the door in her face. Angel allowed this young girl to stay at her home for several weeks, hiding her from her mother, after she learned that she was being physically abused by her mother constantly. Police had been called and child services got involved. The children were threatened to be placed in foster care, and Angel couldn't bear the thought of that happening, so she volunteered to take them all in. At the time, Angel was barely surviving, but she thought that at least the kids would be safe. Unfortunately, it turned out that Angel was not allowed to take them in, but another neighbor who lived down the street from them had the financial means to do so. Angel was able to agree with the neighbor to take in the child that she was already nurturing because she wanted so badly to stay in Angel's home while the other siblings were fine with staying with the neighbor. Years had gone by, and Angel and the young girl that she had taken in somehow lost touch. At the age of 19 years old, the young lady found Angel, and they remained very close. To Angel, it meant a lot that this young lady never forgot about her and that she had made every effort to find her. Until this day, the young lady still calls Angel "mom".

Angel always tried to save men from their hurt pasts. They would always feel so comfortable telling her what their past traumas were, and they loved the fact that she never judged them for it. Angel tried to love the trauma out of them, only to find out that it wouldn't work. She would always tell them that they would be okay, that she loved them, and that they could be anything they wanted to be. She shared encouraging words with them saying that they were good men and to not let their pasts define them. They used Angel to build themselves up while they only tore her down. The same encouragement and love weren't reciprocated by Angel, but a part of that was Angel's fault because she choose these toxic men.

Why not Therapy?

After the rape, Angel went to therapy, but only once. In her mind, it didn't work because, well she and the therapist just didn't relate. She was a textbook therapist who sat with her legs perfectly crossed with a notebook in hand. She spoke like the therapists you see on television. "So, tell me what brings you in today?" "Let me remind you that it's not your fault." Angel would think, "DUH, I know this!" Angel didn't feel like the therapist connected to her at all, so she politely disconnected from the thought of therapy. Angel wanted a genuine therapist for Black families like Angel's, she was taught that therapy made you weak, so that mindset didn't help. She was told that she would and could work it out on her own. In the same way, as men are taught that crying is for the weak; this is why people begin to hold in their feelings while disconnecting from the people that they truly love. Angel believes that this is what happened to her father. His voice and tears were silenced.

She didn't try to find another therapist because she didn't know any better, and her mother didn't force the issue. Angel thought that after so much time had gone by, she could just forget about the rape. For some time, she was able to suppress that incident and move on with her life, but the emotions that were attached to it came out in other ways: anger, fear of abandonment, guilt, frustration, stress, mistrust, and disappointment. She needed to talk to someone about it.

Angel now knows and understands that by getting therapy she would have been able to better heal. She probably wouldn't have accepted or chosen the type of men that she chose and accepted. She wouldn't have had such high expectations of men, and she would have been okay with the disappointments as opposed to expressing anger. She would have learned to forgive in a way that she could let go and let God handle it. Instead, she grew vengeful toward people, especially men. She would make sure that other people felt the same type of hurt and pain that she felt.

Angel's mother would ask her, "Why do you have to get revenge all of the time?" "Because it makes me feel better," Angel would reply. Angel has since learned that therapy helps you to better analyze things and be able to put things into a mature perspective. It is a gem to be able to deal with people and things as they are instead of what you expect them to be. Also, getting therapy from the right therapist can help one to properly heal. She understands this now. Through therapy, Angel also learned that she was searching for a man who was better than her father, but instead, she kept dating her father, and it was making her angrier and angrier.

Me, A Therapist?

Angel never had any intentions of becoming a therapist. It was not until she heard a voice in her sleep directing her to get up that morning and enroll in graduate school as a mental Health Therapist aka Professional Counselor. Angel didn't question God; she did as she was told. To be honest, Angel loved taking courses that helped to understand how the brain works. She loved the idea of being able to help people even though it would be the greatest challenge of her life. How could she be a therapist when she wasn't healed? She still needed therapy herself. Despite it all, she had discovered her purpose.

It took two years of hard work and dedication before graduating with her Master's in Professional Counseling. Angel graduated Sum Cum Laude (with honors), and she was super proud of herself. She stayed up many nights writing 20-page papers on subjects about mental health. She was exhausted but fulfilled. When that day came and her name was called to walk across that stage, it was the proudest moment for her. Angel and her family piled up in one SUV like a bunch of illegal aliens and headed to Virginia from TN. It was a 12-hour drive for Angel to proudly walk across that stage.

She remembers the anxiety that she felt a month prior when she was required to take a test to graduate with her full 60-hour credit. If she failed the test, she would obtain a lesser degree and 30 of her credits would disappear. It was a one-shot test with a "Pass" or "Fail". Angel remembers as she was taking the three-hour test, her palms were sweaty, her hands were shaking, and she felt as though she was going to pass out. As she watched each person finish their test and walk out to hand it to the professor, her anxiety level rose. She found herself close to the last person left to finish the test. Angel wondered why everyone was finishing so quickly. It made her feel dumb. Although Angel was a really smart girl who always made the honor roll throughout her entire life, she always had anxiety when taking tests.

When the test results arrived in the mail, she was afraid to open them. Angel's heart was beating so fast, and she could hardly breathe. She thought, "What if I went through all of that hard work for nothing?" When she opened the envelope and saw a big fat PASS on that letter, Angel cried. She had finally done it! She was going to be a Therapist!

Angel worked as a Master's level therapist for several years. She worked as an independent contractor in low-income communities where the chances of her getting harmed in someone's home or neighborhood was highly likely to happen. After about two years of experience in the industry, she started to ditch the adults (especially males because of her past), to work more closely with children with ADHD, Oppositional Defiance, Depression, Anxiety, and Bipolar Disorder.

Angel would request not to have males placed on her caseload because she didn't want to feel vulnerable while in their homes. She wanted to avoid the googly-eyed broken men who always found her extremely attractive and kind. Her experiences with working with men during therapy sessions were that they would be distracted by her beauty. They would try to flirt or stare at her lustfully rather than focus on their healing. She didn't want to take the chance of getting raped again if they were rejected. At times, it became hard for her to be professional while thinking in the back of her head…"Am I safe?" On the other hand, the women that she dealt with were mostly in their 20's and 30's and dealt with Depression, Anxiety, and Bipolar. They loved her as a therapist.

Some of the women to whom she provided counseling too were dealing with past traumatic experiences such as she did (rape, child molestation, child abuse, and domestic violence). She could especially relate to them, but at the same time, that was not good for her since it was more like a "trigger" for her. As they would speak about their experiences, she would have flashbacks of what happened to her. Angel would take their experiences home with her and sleep with them swirling around in her head. She would hurt them, as she did the same with kids who experienced emotional, sexual, or physical abuse. She would take their burdens home with her. She wanted to save them all. As a therapist, this would be an unhealthy way for her to heal.

The desire to help people came out of her passion for stopping people from going through life guideless as she did. She had always had the desire to help people even when she had earned a degree in Political Science and wanted to go to law school to become an attorney. Call it divine intervention if you pay for her to become a therapist instead. The desire to become an attorney was immediately placed on hold as she heard this strong inner spirit instructing her to study to become a therapist. She didn't question it because knew and felt that it was the voice of God speaking to her. Becoming a therapist was not the journey that Angel chose, but a journey that choose her.

The joy of helping people to overcome their issues was like no other for Angel. Helping others also helped her little by little. Listening, understanding, and being empathetic came naturally to her, but patience was something that she had to learn. Being a therapist taught Angel that patience and forgiveness were needed to heal. Most of the recommendations or advice that she would give to clients would apply to her situation as well, but as a mental health therapist, she was unable to see how to help herself.

BOUNDARIES

Setting boundaries is very important to Angel because it means you get to choose what you want in life and what you don't. Most importantly, you get to choose peace. Angel has learned that you can find peace within yourself by putting yourself first. So, that is why she had to set boundaries with not only her clients but also her own family.

Although Angel had obtained the education and skills to become a therapist, her family showed no respect for it. They would speak as though this was not her profession, and at times would act as though they knew more about her profession than she did. To add insult to injury, they would "google" things regarding therapy and explain different diagnoses as if she did not know the field that she had worked so hard to be a part of. In Angel's mind, this was a form of disrespect. Angel felt that they mocked her and her profession. They simply didn't understand it or her. Angel felt that she was fighting a battle with her family at the risk of her healing.

Burn Out

Being a therapist can be quite challenging, especially if you haven't healed. Your client's problems become your problems. When their anxiety increases, your anxiety increases. Your mental health begins to deteriorate over time. Have you ever seen a show or movie where a psychologist or therapist is talking to a client, and they look as if they have checked out? This is because he or she probably has.

Over time, Angel became burnt out as a therapist. She was taking on more than she could handle. She realized she was demonstrating countertransference- where a therapist begins to show an emotional entanglement with his or her clients once they have attached their feelings to the client's past relationships. She was beginning to feel uncomfortable while the client spoke about their trauma. She would become super emotional or angry with the client. Unbeknownst to Angel, she had taken on the emotions and burdens of her clients.

Ultimately, Angel enjoyed being a therapist, but the burnout was real. After several years in the field, she didn't have the desire to do it anymore. Covid 19 hit the U.S. by surprise, which was the perfect opportunity to exit the field with the "stay at home" order. She had decided not to take the risk of entering into people's homes and catching the Covid 19 virus. She was physically, psychologically, and emotionally tired, so she walked away with the feeling that she had completed a form of stewardship that God set out for her to do.

To her surprise, the experience of working with clients was somewhat therapeutic for her because working with others through that season of their lives helped her to heal in some areas.

A New Venture

Funny how life turns around at a 360-degree angle. passion for hair became a rebirth in the form of a new natural hair care line. While sleeping, she heard a name come into her mind and immediately woke up at 3 a.m. to write the name down so that wouldn't forget it. Several hours later, she was trying to figure out how to register a business as an LLC, ingredients for products, how to find someone to build a website, and where to buy labels and materials. Angel had figured all of these things out on her own, including how to get a business trademarked. Angel's online natural hair growth company, did quite well during the first year of Covid and is still in business. But as with most companies, business owners have their ups and downs. This is entrepreneur life, and regardless of what happens, Angel was determined to stick it out.

Entrepreneurship is something that's embedded in Angel. Her father was an entrepreneur who loved the idea of ownership and not having to answer to anyone. Angel loved the idea of financial freedom and creating generational wealth for her children, grandchildren, and other grandchildren to come. Creating generational wealth is important for the Black community. Her motto is: 1.) Trust in God 2.) Trust in your Purpose 3.) Use the Gifts that God gave you 4.) Always believe in Yourself 5.) Always bet on YOU and manifest the things that you desire.

Angel has thought about going back into therapy. But it would all depend on what God wanted her to do. At this moment, she needed a mental health break of her own. She also needed therapy to completely overcome the things that have gone through in life. Most people wouldn't believe that the therapists, psychologists, and psychiatrists they go to for help are the same people who may need help themselves. In this profession, therapists tend to suppress their "stuff" to help others but are also broken. Therapists sacrifice a lot of themselves so that others can be healed. It's not always okay, but it's God's work.

As a therapist, psychologist, social worker, or any mental health professional, you try to save the world, but the truth is that you can't save everybody. To heal, each person has to put in the work.

Chapter Ten

ADVICE TO YOUNG GIRLS

Daddy Issues

Often, men don't fully understand their impact on their daughters' lives. The role of a father can never be overemphasized. For daughters, a father is the first man in their life. They are the first to show their daughters what love looks like because they give their girls special love and guidance and how they should be treated by other men. That's where the term "daddy's little girl" comes from. From a psychological and emotional perspective, sometimes girls become more connected to their father than to their mother, and then it's vice versa for boys. If a father is not the first man to show and tell his little girl that he loves them, then she may begin to get a false perception of what love from a man looks or feels like.

Angel tossed around the words "I love you" like it was a ball to play with because she didn't take those words seriously or understand what they truly meant. When she said it to men, she didn't mean it. She would only say it if a man told her that he loved her first-Victor was the only exception. Those words "I love you" were a lie because of the hurt from Angel's father and she never believed anything that any man told her. Those words didn't carry much weight with Angel; they only came with disappointment.

Angel considered herself to be perfectly imperfect. A human being who has made many mistakes in her life, and many bad choices when it came to men and relationships. She never understood that her past trauma would impact the narrative of her relationships and that she would continue to attract men who had also experienced mommy and daddy issues. It's called "trauma bonding". Trauma bonding is unhealthy, and once recognized, you should immediately disconnect from that person. It is okay to be by yourself to heal. Two unhealed individuals cannot help one another. You cannot love the trauma out of someone. He or she has to be willing to go to therapy, pray, and do the work that is needed to properly heal. Stop ignoring the red flags, just so that you can stay in a relationship. Learn to love yourself first. You are important, and you should be valued every single day. If you are in a domestic situation, get out. Go to a safe place, Stop making excuses for your abuser. Stop allowing him or her to think that it is okay to harm you in any form or fashion because it's never okay.

God, The Perfect Father Figure

Angel used to envy those little girls who had loving fathers in their lives because she missed out on having one. Now, she sees those little girls as blessed to have their fathers and she prays that there will be more fathers brave enough to step up to the plate for their little girls. Although Angel's father never stepped up to the plate, God did. And because of that Angel considers herself very blessed. God showed Angel love, patience, and understanding. He kept her strong and held her when she needed him to. Each time Angel can open her eyes to see another day, she thanks God for that opportunity. It's an opportunity to love, learn, and live. But there were many challenges that Angel experienced before she learned to truly surrender to God's rule over her life.

Advice

It's not worth it to harbor all of that anger inside you because it is going to manifest somewhere else, and the outcome is never good. Women who are in prison now are linked to hurt that was inflicted by a man. Whether they were vulnerable enough to carry drugs for them or if there was a domestic violence dispute and they ended up in jail because they had to stab or shoot him, it was unresolved anger that caused them to be sent to prison. Don't allow that anger and pain to control you; it will do more harm than good.

Embrace the healing process in your life by doing things that will bring you peace. Journaling is one tool in the healing process and Angel always emphasizes the power of prayer and meditation on God's word.

Staying close to God helps in the healing process; pouring your heart out, even with tears, is very helpful in your restoration process.

NEW RESOLUTION

Today, Angel is choosing to have a voice and then be a voice of healing for women. She wants to encourage them to refrain from being reckless. Before she became a therapist, she was reckless and only made bad choices with men.

Habakkuk Cooper

Today, Angel recommends walking away from troubled men. Choose yourself first. Make deposits within yourself before making them for other people because you may not get a valid receipt from others. People will never value you until you show them how much you value yourself.

Speak to My Healing

FINAL THOUGHTS

O ur ability to experience pain is one thing that unites us as humans. Many people have been harmed, whether it's physically, mentally, or emotionally. What distinguishes us is how we react to our past trauma. Pain is part of life; it must be embraced and measured for good. There will be situations in life that may be way beyond our control.

When emotional distress keeps you from recuperating from a scenario, experts have discovered that it's an indication that you're not going ahead with a growth-oriented approach.

One of the most potent and time-tested methods to recover from difficulty is to take the lessons learned and apply them to future growth and progress. If we get stuck thinking about what "could have been, we might get weakened by terrible sensations and memories.

You should also know that healing begins with you; you have to accept the fact that your trauma exists and don't live in self-denial.

Don't substitute God with people; there are things in life only God can supply. Don't look for validation from fellow human beings. Your self-identity, esteem, and purpose come from God. His love for you is eternal and unconditional.

He is your source. His thought towards you are thoughts of good and not evil.

Forgiveness is also very important in the healing process; you have to let go and let God. Forgiveness aids in your ability to move on to better days ahead of you.

You are no longer a victim but a victory, don't stay attached to the pain; with God, it will turn into your gain.

If you're trying to move on from a distressing situation but don't know where to begin, here are a few suggestions to get you started:

1. Create a positive mantra to help you overcome your negative ideas

Your self-talk may either propel you ahead or keep you stranded. In emotional distress, having a mantra to repeat to oneself may often help you reframe your ideas.

"Can't believe this happened to me!" says clinical psychologist Carla Manly, Ph.D., instead of getting involved. "I am lucky to discover a new route in life — one that is excellent for me," says a positive mantra.

2. Establish physical separation

It's fairly unusual to hear someone advise you to keep your distance from the person or circumstance that is bothering you.

According to clinical psychologist Raman Durvasula, Ph.D., that isn't such a horrible notion. "Creating physical or psychological space between ourselves and the person or circumstance might aid in letting go since we don't have to think about, process, or be reminded of it as much," she adds.

3. Work independently

It is critical to focus on oneself. You might choose whether or not to face the pain you've felt. Bring yourself back to the present whenever you think about someone who has brought you sorrow. Then focus on something for which you are grateful. This is like shifting to your happy place.

4. Become more aware

According to Lisa Olivera, a registered marital and family therapist, the more we can focus on the current moment, the less influence our past or future has on us.

"When we practice being present, our wounds lose their power over, and we have greater flexibility to choose how we want to respond to our life."

5. Be kind to yourself. Self-love is the greatest kind of love

If you find yourself in self-blame for not being able to let go of an unkind circumstance, it's time to treat yourself with respect and compassion.

This, according to Olivera, is treating oneself as we would a friend, practicing self-compassion, and avoiding making comparisons to others' experiences.

"Hurt is unavoidable, and we may not be able to prevent it, but we can choose to treat ourselves with kindness and love when it happens."

6. Allow unpleasant feelings to surface

Don't worry if you ignore bad feelings because you're afraid of them. You're not alone. In fact, according to Durvasula, many individuals are terrified of emotions like sorrow, rage, disappointment, or melancholy.

People attempt to block them out rather than feel them, which can sabotage the process of letting go. "These unpleasant feelings are riptides," Durvasula explains. "Allow them to pour out of you... It may necessitate mental health treatment, but battling them might trap you," she says.

7. You must choose to live with the other person who will not apologize

Your healing process will be slowed if you wait for an admission of guilt from the person who has injured you. If you've been harmed or are in agony, it's critical that you take care of yourself, which may involve understanding that the person who has hurt you may not apologize.

8. Practice self-care.

When we are in pain, it might seem like there is nothing but pain. Setting boundaries, saying no, doing the things that bring joy and comfort, and listening to our own needs first, are all examples of self-care.

"The more self-care we can incorporate into our day-to-day life, the more empowered we will feel." "Our hurts don't feel as overpowering from there," she says.

9. Hang out with folks who make you happy.

This simple yet effective strategy can help you through a lot of pain. As Manly argues, we can't do life alone and certainly can't expect to get through our pains alone. "Allowing ourselves to depend on loved ones for support is such a fantastic method of not just minimizing loneliness, but also reminding of the good in our life."

10. Permit yourself to discs it.

Permitting yourself to talk about uncomfortable feelings or a scenario that has caused you distress is critical.

According to experts, people sometimes can't let go because they don't feel they can talk about it. "This might be because their friends and family don't want to hear about it anymore, or [the individual] feels embarrassed or humiliated to talk about it," she says.

However, it is critical to talk about it. That's why an expert suggests finding a buddy or therapist who can be a sounding board and is patient and accepting.

11. Allow yourself to forgive yourself.

You may need to focus on your forgiveness since waiting for the other person to apologize might prolong the process of letting go.

Forgiveness is essential to the healing process because it helps you to let go of anger, guilt, shame, grief, or any other negative emotion and go on.

12. Seek professional assistance

If you're having trouble letting go of a traumatic incident, seeking professional help may be beneficial. It can be tough to put these suggestions into practice on your own, so you'll need the assistance of an experienced specialist.

Speak to My Healing

13 COMPELLING REASONS TO PURSUE COUNSELING

1. Something in your life is causing you difficulty

Have you ever felt that you couldn't describe how you're feeling or what you're going through? One of the first signs that someone could benefit from therapy, according to Chase T. M. Anderson, M.D., M.S., a child and adolescent resident in the UCSF Department of Psychiatry, is if they continue to remark, "wish had the words for this," or "need to speak this out more." Both can benefit from therapy. According to experts' opinion, it provides a safe environment for patients to work through their feelings, ideas, and difficult situations' expert tells SELF that "occasionally something very useful comes from this process—becoming a more conscious and better version of ourselves."

"Therapy may be a mirror to hold up to help you view yourself a bit more correctly through the eyes of someone trained to see you fully,". This is especially helpful for getting over our narrow, tunnel-vision view of who we are and what we are going through.

2. Your temper seems to be shorter than normal, and it's influencing your mood, relationships, and other aspects of your life

Are you more quickly irritated by your friends or family over "little" issues? Is your inbox making you more irritated with each passing day? Paying attention to how you react to everyday stressors—and how that has changed over time—can be helpful when deciding whether therapy is right for you.

This includes keeping track of any significant changes in your mood, behaviors, sleep, relationships, decision-making, and your relationship with food, alcohol, or drugs. Some of these may be symptoms of a certain kind of mental health disorder like anxiety or depression, but therapy does not need

108

to be that severe to be potent. Therapy can help sort out some of the foundational causes of these reactions by dealing with the thoughts or feelings at the root of them and the patterns triggering them. You might also learn to incorporate more adaptive coping skills so that, for example, you don't always turn to a drink at the end of a stressful workday.

3. You don't feel like you're operating at full capacity...or even close to it

We can all feel sad, angry, or tired, but it doesn't always affect our lives, relationships, or objectives. According to a psychologist, a change in our optimal functioning is a red flag that we need help. "If getting out of bed feels like a ton of bricks is lying on you, or you're agitated at everyone while running errands," "Right, there is data." It enables you to say, "Hmmm, I'm not feeling as well as I use to, and I'm not doing the things use to like as easily."

According to experts, fluctuations in our mood or worry may impair our focus, decision-making, and even memory, affecting our capacity to complete tasks. Therapy can assist you in determining why these changes have happened and how to return to a more optimum functioning state. For instance, if you're having challenges getting out of bed, you could use the behavioral activation technique to schedule pleasurable activities throughout your day to motivate you.

4. You could talk to someone objectively and confidential

People often compare talking to a therapist to talking to a friend, but this is not the case. A therapist is objective and neutral, does not become exhausted or burdened by your visits, and can completely treat your information privately. Dr. Anderson of the University of Michigan adds, "We have no hidden purpose or prejudiced aspirations; we just want the best for you." "We assist you, the expert in all things you, in delving into the inner workings of your body, mind, and spirit to try to iron out those wrinkles." We don't always provide recommendations or explain what to do; instead, we help to summarize, repeat, or connect some of the information you've shared with ."

This is not the kind of conversation you'd have with a friend. Maybe you want to talk to a friend about these issues, but you don't feel supported by your family—or you've tried to talk to them about it, and they've been unhelpful. According to clinical and forensic psychologist Angela Lawson, Ph.D., associate professor of psychiatry at Northwestern University's Feinberg School of Medicine, "all of these are signs that you might benefit from talking through your situation with a therapist."

5. You're in a rut

Many of the therapists interviewed suggested that therapy can help when you feel unfulfilled, stagnant, or stuck in your life. "You don't feel better even though you have a beyond average zeal to feel better emotionally, or you might even be trying out new behaviors to help yourself feel better, but nothing seems to be working,"

Therapists can help you get freed by helping you figure out your desires as well as any anxieties and fears that may be holding you back. Therapy is also useful for specifying obstacles to joy and getting guidance for overcoming those obstacles."

6. Your life appears to be repeating itself

This differs from feeling stuck because it refers to a certain behavior that you can't manage to break. An expert explains, "One sign you hear often is repeatedly engaging in a behavior that the person can intellectually recognize isn't helpful or healthy, but they find themselves doing it anyway to their disadvantage, whether it's professional, personal, or relationally."

Breaking old behaviors and building new ones, according to Barkholtz, requires objective external help, such as a therapist. "We sometimes don't know there are foundations, contributing causes, and underlying patterns until someone else helps delve a bit deeper, which a therapist is trained to accomplish."

7. You're feeling drained

According to Barkholtz, overwhelm is a big and broad sign that therapy might be beneficial for you because being overwhelmed can be caused by a variety of factors, including relationships and external circumstances, as well as your own emotions. She adds that we typically can't absorb and cope with things when we're overwhelmed, but a therapist can help accomplish both.

Therapy can assist you in learning to name, identify, and comprehend all of your feelings. For example, perhaps you've recently been overcome with rage and irritability, which is certainly not uncommon these days. Dr. Gordon notes, "Mental health specialists assist in identifying the environmental and internal variables that contribute to irritation." "Is it, for example, worry or stress causing it?" Is it necessary to advance communication? Do you need to take supplementary self-care breaks to reduce your anxiety? Therapy is a method of improving your well-being and relationships by teaching you how to deal with tough feelings and situations."

8. Your best isn't enough

You're dealing with unrealistic expectations, such as the need to be continually productive. Expert asserts that even well-functioning high achievers who can go about their daily activities without interruptions might benefit from treatment. "These folks have often learned the value of self-control and responsibility," she adds, "but there may be too much of a good thing." "People with unyielding self-expectations frequently believe that they can never relax, and that life offers too little joy. They may even feel lonely since they believe they can only show people the successful and responsible part of themselves."

Therapy can help you develop a better work-life balance, set boundaries, and learn to connect with people. Perhaps most importantly, it can help you appreciate the flaws that make us human. Dr. Gordon says that therapy may provide strategies to deal with self-criticism and demanding demands.

9. You're planning a significant life change or are already undergoing one

We are often afraid of change, such as relocating, beginning school, or starting a new career. Many people are probably worried about returning to work, if we haven't already, or adjusting to whatever this "new normal" looks like right now.

Therapy may be a useful tool for helping you through these significant adjustments, so you don't have to go it alone.

"Therapy provides an objective, outside perspective on your ideas, feelings, and emotions to help you feel less frightened and overwhelmed about change or transition," says Nia Noire Therapy + Wellness CEO Jessica Gaddy Brown. It assists you in anticipating what to expect and ensuring a smooth transition when the shift occurs. Furthermore, problems and changes will always occur, and understanding how to deal with them now will be beneficial in the future.

"Life will always give you a curveball," Wise adds, "and society has normalized dysfunctional functioning owing to the stigma of mental illness." "How do you maintain your equilibrium despite the curveballs?" One solution is to gain self-awareness and coping skills through counseling.

10. You had a traumatic encounter

Many of you have been affected by tragedies beyond our control, including death, accidents, assault, and bullying, to name a few. Trauma can interfere with our ability to function in interpersonal relationships, be triggered at any moment (including years later), and even appear physically. According to Brown, " therapy can "help you understand your emotional and/or psychosomatic reaction to triggers, [and] give opportunity for clarity and behavior/thought adjustment," according to Brown.

Process racial trauma and microaggressions with a culturally sensitive therapist who helps you feel secure, seen, and heard. "Having someone who is trained to talk through such difficulties, to listen, and to aid is crucial for a minoritized person to thrive in our environment."

11. You want assistance with tough family or interpersonal issues

Current and past family issues are wonderful topics for discussion in therapy, whether in an individual or group context. For example, in individual therapy, you might talk about your relationships to better understand the root causes of some of your behavioral patterns and learn how to navigate those relationships healthy with boundaries and improved communication skills.

If you're battling a specific issue or fighting or any form of strain in your relationship, it might be good to seek objective help from family or couples counseling. Brown explains, "A professional family/couple's therapist can enable effective discourse and problem-solving among family members to improve interpersonal communication and behavioral patterns." "Many individuals find family/couples therapy helpful in repairing parent-child or sibling relationships, guiding new parents through postpartum issues, or assisting couples in enriching their love, resulting in healthier, more loving surroundings."

12. You suffer from a bodily ailment

We often divide the mind and body, perceiving mental disease as distinct from physical sickness. It isn't. Dr. McCabe notes that "injury and disease influence us in many ways—practical, emotional, and social." "We may need to make big lifestyle changes, adopt new coping mechanisms, and deal with significant uncertainty."

POEMS FOR
MY CHILDREN

"Son"

My First Born, My First Crush

It's True

Even Before I laid eyes on you

You Gave me butterflies, No lie

Wait! I'm about to be a mother? A Gift like no other

Oh God...Love at First Sight

What more could a mother ask for?

I absolutely A-DORE you!

My Son, My Hero

Speak to My Healing

You Stole my heart

When God created you, He created such an art

Such a perfectly imperfect creation who was born from me

I thank God for you and love you unconditionally

My Son,

I watched you Grow over the years

While YOU watched my imperfections, trauma, pain, tears

I will always and forever love you, son.

No matter what mistakes are made,

You never judged me, instead, you let me Be

Just your mother.

My Son,

In my eyes, you will always be perfect,

And I am so honored that God gave you to me.

I just want you to be all that you can and want to be.

My Son, My First Born, My First Crush, My King,

You will Always & Forever be EVERYTHING to Me!

" Mini Me" (For my daughter)

If I could describe the perfect Angel,

It would be YOU.

I had no clue,

That God would bless me with the perfect daughter.

My daughter, my mini-me.

Remember the times that we would walk together while holding your hand?

And people would stare?

They would smile and say, girl...that's you're "mini ".

I wouldn't dare trade you for the world

Because you're SO much more.

knew when you were born, that had finally done everything right

For the first time in my life, I didn't have to fight

Fears of looking for love in all the wrong faces

Because your love took me to much higher places

My Mini Me, My Bestie

You stuck with me through thick and thin

Speak to My Healing

Even when I made terrible choices with men

When he mistreated me, you reminded me that I deserved better

And even when I knew that past pain wouldn't let me move forward.

But now that I have you, I feel free enough to teach you how to better spread your wings

So that you can be the better version of ME

Because of you, I am a lot stronger

Even though it may have taken just a little bit longer

My Mini me

I'm so happy to be your mother

And I pray that you never experience the hurt and pain that I have,

You deserve to be forever loved by ME

And I promise that I got you

I love you...

Unconditionally

My Mini Me

If you liked this book or found it helpful, I'd appreciate it if you could leave a quick review on Amazon. Your support is greatly appreciated. All of the reviews will be read to obtain your feedback and improve the book.

Thanks for your help and support!

Speak to My Healing

Therapy Chapter

HARD TIMES

A. The Struggle

For her siblings, the story was not different; we all had our fair share of the traumatic experience, and none of them discussed it; we all kept it to ourselves; believing that made it worse. believe not talking makes the pain linger for a longer time.

Communicating, especially with people who can relate to your pain, is key to healing.